Hope in the Heart of Hatred

Twenty-nine poems

HOPE
IN THE
HEART
OF
HATRED

Writing No.8

PETER HAGUE

First Published in 2021
by Peter Hague Concept Design Art Direction

ISBN 978-1-8382746-0-3

Cover Design, layout and typography:
Peter Hague Concept Design Art Direction.

Photographs by Peter Hague.
Other photography by Lara Newton.

Also available in paperback: ISBN 978-1-8382746-1-0

A catalogue record for this book
is available from the British Library.

To those patient –
who wait so long they begin to weep –
firstly from their eyes
and later from the heart.

6

Peter Hague 1994

Introduction by the Author

This book of collected poems was written between 1989 and 2003, a period when I was a freelance designer, eventually working on a private museum project. I continued to write throughout this period – not only these poems, but short stories and other writings too – not to mention continuing a lifelong fascination with creative photography, the echoes of which are ghosted here. However, it is poetry that has always been a consistent foundation in my life – certainly since my early twenties, when drawn into the magic of writing through such diverse poets as Kathleen Raine, Leonard Cohen and T. S. Eliot.

The mood of the poems contained in this book is somewhat different to those from the previous decades of my life, and also to the style I write in now. They represent what might be called a 'bridging period', spanning the millennium and reaching back. It seems therefore right that this short collection enters the public arena now – offering a tantalising introduction to myself and my earlier work. I have also added some of my photography, not particularly in support of the poems, but purely offering their own form of ambience to my personal history – that of the 'poet' who has spent a lifetime in the service of art and design – a period one might almost call a predisposition.

In fact, there is a mild bitterness about these poems, sometimes bordering on cynicism – but it is a tooled bitterness, sharpened to provide explanation and reason – certainly more so than my previous collection from the nineteen eighties, which was notably edgy. There are many moments of softness and humour here too. I think this mood came from my age at the time – being mostly in my forties and still trying to find a useful direction – a self-exiled wanderer, trapped inside his own talent and trying to steer it through what seemed a bitter and relentless trial.

While designing this book and editing these poems, some twenty years later, I have been careful not to disturb the fundamental feelings of nagging disappointment, which is probably at their heart. In some ways, I found it easy to re-enter those difficult times with a similar mood, possibly conjured from the anxieties and disappointments of the present. There was also a danger of submitting to depression – a darkness no doubt fuelled from the same underlying explorations of bitterness and guilt that had originally stirred my heart to write these concessions.

There are some interesting ideas in this book – also some revelations and confessions, and it certainly holds its place amongst my much older work and also the poems I am writing at the present time – some of which have been posted on social media and are also to be published in my forthcoming anthology entitled: 'Gain of Function'.

I think 'Hope in the Heart of Hatred', the title chosen back in the 1990s for this 'bridging book', still speaks for itself – for it is a book truly concerned with the possibilities for hope, without shying away from the fact that hatred, heartache and evil, are insidious in our world and play against our best efforts on a daily basis.

Peter Hague 2021

HOPE
IN THE
HEART
OF
HATRED

Camouflage

Ladies and Gentlemen! We are about to go onstage –
bending make-up over broken skin,
with the effort of a reluctant voyager
trying to close a suitcase that has far too much within.
This is a performance in itself,
so appreciate our efforts and the risks involved –
we may not be top-drawer,
but a surplus of lust at least aspires
to the lewdest beckonings of the worst top shelf.
And do not mind if our manners come adrift,
failing standards from time to time...
and try to avert your eyes
should we lean too far, or you feel offended.
In reparation, I urge you to laugh if we get up-ended.

We have a real 'off-stage' suitcase too.
It is over-burdened with fabric remedies –
the hats and clothes for the ailing shape.
And just in case nothing suits,
we can always throw about these intemperate bones...
'The Cape' – the last resort – the actors' folly –
a foil designed to take the edge off the naked ape.

We will no-doubt use camouflage and some sticky tape –
for the misplaced thoughts our orchestra reveals:
That sad beauty, which finally shames us.

Still Looking

I want to be normal again and watch Beverly Hills Cop.
Me! Making a bust on my own TV.
Confining the forbidden fruit of relentless stardom
to my treacherous larder –
as good as any rehabilitation and perhaps harder...
something to flush down the toilet
of the next half-hour –
when the television police arrive
to plant their schedule inside my clock.

I want to be normal again... if I ever was?
Especially now I have seen the tight, white pants of fame
walk out into that flashing world –
relentless minders fastened like bullets around a belt.
Having a remote control might also help?
Just incase I go too far –
incase I suddenly need to watch
the other side of myself.

I cannot wear the uncreased image
of double-breasted suits;
my head sticks out and makes no sense.
Something like a mop, dejected in a corner –
soothed only by water and dripping wet –
the sure smell of disinfectant
becoming a perfect ounce of regret.

No one can wear big suits anymore.
Not and escape the persistent enquiry that follows.
Not without slicking back their careless hair
beyond sensible recognition –

perhaps showing a daring moustache
with their lover's permission?
Or trimming their personality
down to the merest back and sides.

A good suit wears the skin itself –
promoting its empathy with comfortable precision.
Our scraggy human form
is nothing like its tailored master,
and is kept out of sight –
except for the flash of sudden feet.
These are allowed to wallow, sockless in conceit,
wearing white painted slip-on shoes –
a ploy to prove there is someone inside
this unpromising sense of bearing.

Otherwise, the body is sterilised,
under a profusion of camouflage dressings –
preferably made dead – stifled, or mummified.

I could never venture out onto the stage alone.
I would always require the attention
of a companion, or a nurse:
There at the mercy of the footlights
they announce my verse...

> *'And now, we would like to present...*
> *The mysterious Peter Hague – star and coat hanger.*
> *Not necessarily hung in the correct order.'*

Home

I will dip my face in the cool, dark earth
and escape the screaming suburb world.
Or close the office blind
and shut their stormy faces out –
out from inside my fractured mind.
There is a street beyond here
that we have made ruthless and unkind.

After the rain in the soapy evening,
when the tired worker – tired of his job,
hauls himself in from his dreams with a net.
Laying them aside, like toys he is tired of –
or the burden he is tired of,
having let them all down –
having let slip their ambition of noble spectre –
having closed their chapter in his stilted book.
He transfixes himself, drinking television and beer,
wearing his special seat and his uncontested crown –
sighing for ghosts in an absence of love.

It is as practical a stance as he can maintain,
suspending his longing by an invisible strain.
But dreams should never be put into jars
just because we are home
and live on Mars.

A New Lover?

Only when waking at the mouth of a river,
where the sea sucks all day at England's juices,
can a new turmoil of life be rolled out –
out of this old stance of living bones –
these translucent cages that swear they can float
in the flowing camouflage of a furtive note.
They tempt you to forget your past lovers
and begin again – starting with a haircut
or a newer coat.

Only the mist, or the veil of raining salt persist.
Thrown by the wind onto dry, quiet lips.
They sting like a handful of gritty days
and confuse the confusion of unsettled love –
those half-remembered, long-lost ways.

Only these strained roots can recapture desire,
teasing with their current hand of living fire...
to sail you out onto the sea once more
and to further heartache
stroked pure, by waves.

The Perfection of Memory

If you leave me I will stop –
caught like a ship, by rock.
Left alone by the refusing wind
on an unwilling ocean of stilled pretend.
Only the invisible sun
will light my strange, new boredom –
an empty bowl of sky
where a moon means nothing.

With you the sea is infinite.
With you the sea is willing.
But if you leave me, I will stop.
And with everywhere to go
I will go nowhere –
a ship, beached or caught by rock.
I will be barely able to roll with a wave
or roll on a sock,
or comb my hair in a useful way.
I will wait with lowered eyes –
confused and hollow –
tainted by my own coward lies...
where you are still perfect
in my forgiving memory.

An Eternity of Horror Comes to an End

Gather the dead of every death
and tell them death is over.
Those once drowned,
who swim forever in a vast human shoal –
gather them in – it is time!
Those passing blind
through the colourless mist –
gather them in this time.

Gather the murdered, who hide in crowds
from the deliberate feet of passing killers.
Gather those from the blood of war,
who march forever, far on far.

And gather the children of the monster's want –
dirtied by an urge they did not understand.
Gather them back to the arms of your love
and show them their killers serve nothing but time,
in the dry agony of unspendable tears.

Gather death from its own darkness
and squeeze out a life from its returning sense of home,
saying: 'The end is the beginning, so do not roam.
You have waited forever for this, we know,
but the universe was barred by destruction too,
and by gods who stood in the way.
We can only apologise for the persistence of truth.
If there is anything else we can do, just say.'

The Ghost of Aggression

His eyes were filled with a familiar pain,
which spread into his face down lines of flesh
and told his history at a glance.

The sky held a dull promise of rain,
blowing friendless wind at the rattling pane.
I read the palm of his open expression
and asked him (while knowing):
'What troubles you now... or troubles you again;
is it the ravenous ghost of futile aggression?
Has it grown too pale for even lament,
or is it now just a dark obsession?
Does it live in these ragged lines, sharpened by light?
Does it snipe instead, with a hollow bullet?
A tear in the brass eye of a leaving lover?
Or from suddenly concerned, yet camouflaged friends,
who deny they know you, now the war is over?'

He died in my arms, without real comfort –
only the pleasure of his sacrifice.

More Make Up

On concrete, beneath the pouring sun
the paper clown lays still as a gun,
but with the silence and knowing
of trees and stars –
and the dormant impartiality of fun.

Voices have left on childrens' feet
and echo into the files of Lister Street.
They said goodbye for the call of television...
and for the sake of sounding incomplete.

And now the wind has told the clown
that all is lost to the staring frown.
And all is blind to the staring eye,
as the clown flies into an empty sky.

Spinning and spinning in a power of flight –
excused in the shades of fading light.
He leaves his children for a another week.
Vision blurred, in the corner of an eye.

Where Does His Genius End?

It ends where the flame
has ignited every private moment
and burnt it to death.
It ends where his family suffered
through the search for illumination
and a meaningful breath.

It ends in darkness –
where bitter went to spend itself,
in the cold of an endless waste.
It ends in the irony of a trapped smile
on that frozen tundra of the face.

It ends beyond the sacrifice of the self,
where the tired publisher's mighty eye
fails to detect a phrase in common
and casts it to the bracken of the godless heath.
It ends with the rejection of an abandoned king,
whose queen advanced life's slice of cake,
but not the reality to bake it in.
(though hers was proven
in the better bakery of belief)

It ends between the awful border
of her unkind slice –
the blade that she and we
and all the burden of our various fates
will one day lay beneath.

Glue

I fell into a hobby shop one broken day
to see the shelves where I used to play.
And there among the ships and planes
were the plastic pieces of our remains.

And many other displaced delights
cleft from the weave of enchanting nights.
I found a model of our relationship
when it was true and watertight.

I finally modelled myself – a clown –
in thirty pieces – broken down.

I bore no colours that hope might wear,
but being the monochrome of true despair,
I felt it likely I would resolve myself here –
bathed in the noble healing of repair.

Tea Time Food Chain

The afternoon birds
melt into the washbowl of evening.
Calling the dark an evil black breath
even their raven wings cannot match.
Nor the beak of prodding death,
pecking holes in the backbone sky –
making stars to light their runway home.

Diminishing echoes cross the rose river,
pulsing like sonar through each quivering feather.
Vibrating in the subtle language of wind and bone,
while wheels spin home to cushioned rooms
filled with gloss and anguish.

More death has been counted in these miles of food
than any mouth dare say –
they chop the liver anyway, as the starving train
rumbles its bulging stomach home.

Screams are softer and more frightening
in the smothering folds of a creased suit...
or a stilted frown...
or a powdered cheek...
and worrying messages lurk, submerged,
in the lips of blood-stained lipstick-speak.

Lips and minds that frown together –
commuted sighs that bind together –
all these eliminated souls, that shuffle
beneath the farmyard cost of human beings –
beneath the pigswill and the cow peeing.

They yearn for faces to break a smile
in some long, future moment of the next mile –
but the green acres where our joys graze
are stained in the blood of market days,
or rumoured lost between guiding rails
and the lean beauty of our parallel plays.

These are troubled actors, travelling too late
to unwind the tightly coiled spring
of their registered, but obscure fate.
And with no will to push against the silver spoon
that casually flicks them beyond all privilege –
home, to the edge of the plate.

Walking On Your Own Grave

The future will despise you
after you have burned
all the things it needed.
Used them so badly
they had to be buried
in a concrete box.

'Made dark,' you said, in a coded way –
so they could not burn back.
At least not until you, yourself were dead
and had your lousy day.

There is still a future in prediction, though,
and enough serious waste in the mulching sea,
for tomorrow to be cast in honesty and truth,
and as bleak as you always deny it will be.

You yearn to be remembered in the register of progress,
leaving some kind of gesture, or indelible mark –
like a statue or an equation – or a glorious beacon,
shining out across the far fields of the dark...
but what good light will seek an overcast face
when you have poisoned your own spark?

Your child is the skin of your future.

Live Performance

We can live if we want to –
right up until the Sun explodes.
We can live in joyful dirt, like toads...
but only till the Sun explodes.

It will burn us into a blackness, then,
without true form or consequence –
yet a cloud that needs no biological glue
to bond that eternal persistence:
the cosmic essence of me and you.

We are small enough to start again –
cleansed into the comfortable shape

of nothing.

Dark Glasses At Fifty Paces

A dark glass duel beneath the sun
is always taking place somewhere in the world.
At every moment, here and there,
the combatants willpower is struck dumb –
stuck and hung
on the blunt end of physical attraction.

So why not here and now?
Why should the shielded, soft eyes
of fragile men and women
not be charging each other with the electric looks
of promised lust and agitation?
At least for the dark age of the next half-hour –
boosting each other with the blush of power
and the cosmetic surgery of practical service.

There is a longing here:
filling our souls with purpose and desire –
relieving the inner motor of the heart
of its dull, monotonous choir.

For one moment we are alive again,
before the impaling glance of a lover's mime
is thrust through our practised heads,
pinning our living logic to an instance of time.
But that is for the future... not yours or mine.

Let us kiss; let me nudge your thighs apart.
Let me pull you willingly onto my automatic heart.
Let me drape you like the flag of victory –
a lotion smoothed across a sun-stripped body,

feeling the ludicrous reaction of my pole of worship
until it wilts like a daisy in your blooming vase.

But first, let us have tea and talk and explain ourselves.
To see if we have any common ground to lay upon –
something to get revitalised about –
something to argue passionately about,
using the weapons of etiquette and kisses.

Let us smudge our eyes with dark glass
and live in the smouldering hope
of uniting our privacy.

Much Later and Alone

My conscience would be happier
doing other things inside my room,
but my business nudges me, like a thorny crown.
I cannot unsnag my leisure from paranoia and fear.
Even on holiday, I am impaled on prices,
and how expensive or cheap the drinks are here –
I am stuck on decisions of wanting or not,
in my hopeless turn of disarray.
Will it cloud my sky for the rest of the day?

Can I afford this sandy beach
to run through my fingers – an irritation of time?
I have become an hourglass: an egg-clock –
that restricted shape is undeniably mine.
And I have all the implications of ticking concern
that surround the importance of a clock's measure.
Work is poking at my pendulum brain,
but if I go to it now it will not swing clear –
I would be out of the window with my eyes and mind –
in the disloyal catchment of ultimate dismay.

This striped chair is all that proves I exist
in a universe fuelled by permanent decay.
Otherwise, I would be falling to Earth
with my absent dreams and thoughts of death.
My dreams absconded twenty years ago
via the exhausted conduit of an eager breath.

The skin of this chair thrusts me skyward –
pushing me upward from these patio slabs.
We are an equilibrium of gravitational force

that some would call a holiday in itself.
I am lofted like a sacrifice to a futile god,
who is only worshipped by selfish thoughts,
and has ceased to exist behind a local Sun
for unworthy girls and boys like me.
We rarely turn to the power of prayer –
we followers of nothing but vacuous joy.
And our following fails in our home regions too –
gods cannot shine on a land of frowns.

Are gods just a series of preferred pronouns?
Or do they, in their sense of being, have true gender?
Is 'He', anything we cannot properly address,
or perhaps a 'She', we can't quite remember?

Holy Spirit, may I pray now,
without attracting the anger of your enemies?
I have enough coping with the scorn of my friends,
and life is hard, pretending to be me.
Kneeling like a disciple on these hot, ceramic tiles.
I cannot bare the struggle with next door's religion,
there is a shared anxiety in our elaborate smiles.

Lord, I have done my best.
My clients think I am Jesus Christ –
I am both revered and persecuted in the same breath.

> *Heaven in art, which father our.*
> *My dog is a god.*
> *I pray backwards.*

The Heart of Hatred

Deep in the heart of Texas
is a cowboy we all love.
He showed us how to wear a gun
that we would never need to use.
He told us how to look at men
so our eyes disarmed the fuse –
and he told us how to kill the bitch
who pissed upon our shoes.

Deep in the heart of hatred
is an envy made of want,
that licks our little, wicked bones
that stick out, thin and gaunt.
We never feed our hatred much
it makes the hunger worse –
we ignore it, with our passing days
until we need a nurse.

Girl On a Wall

Seeing you there was a shock –
in comfortable Lincolnshire.
Beautiful and strong
in the grime of Main Street.
A mask, smoothed tight
across a soul of overwhelming features –
a look that made me want to make something else –
to make something of myself.

In the heart of all difficulty
you seemed life's easy.

Seeing you there –
sitting on a wall and waiting for what?
Is all a man or designer needs
to draw the layout of his life
in an exceptional way –
to put a face to it.

Aimed at Our Head

The wind blows hollow in the drains and pipes,
like thoughts and feelings
sliding inside my prompted soul.
Not stopping at anything I could recall,
but rolling like a pinball through a dark machine –
a silent factory I cannot light, nor more control.

Where are the buffers of my conscience?
I can no longer be the wayward of this secret path.
It was steered away by the express of truth,
but is said to linger in a searching heart.
This path is treacherous; this path is dark –
it has fallen from its game into some far off night,
parachuting deep, like a penetrating thought.
I think it heard the song of some beseeching voice
that sang hollow in the bone of a beguiling flute –
and being an instrument of deception and desire,
this charmed night was deemed a liar,
and outside the rules of our noble house.

I needed the credibility of another mission.
So I applied to my Captain to ask what I could do.
                He said:
'Let the world splash its ideas across your canvas face,
and let some new ideas be cast by you.'

In the end, I could only hear
the eternal language of fear and exchange.
It was forever filled with the unbinding words:
'replace', 'renew', 'recreate', 'rearrange'...
these were sown as seeds into my fallow ear

but grew into frosted chains and legislation.

Who needs a new mission now,
to creep inside this artist-heart?
We all know our stupid fate,
with its discarded secrets and broken faith –
its huge amounts of apathy and waste.
Who needs it now, knowing death is assured?
And blood is the only prize to be poured
on the imminent replacement of our civilised years –
the bullet of acceptance, dividing our eyes.

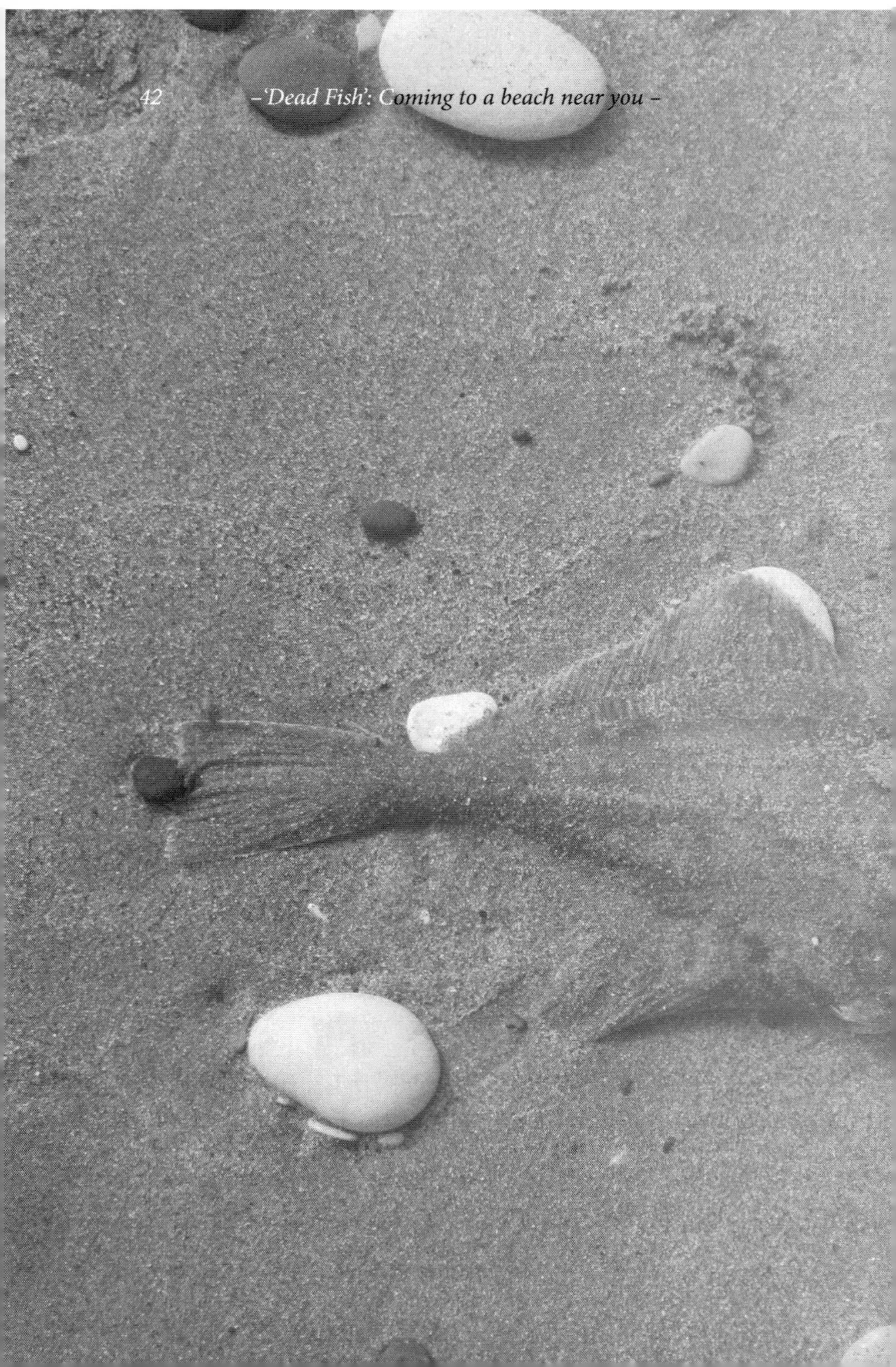

The Revenge of Dead Fish

I see the unfathomable pass my Life.
Do you see them pass yours? Not like me –
my window is shoals of bitterness and loss...
and a measure of pity, to a small degree.

I offered something beyond fried fish,
but realised its sympathy had gorged on their souls;
serving the easier bread of simplified minds,
where oiled sustenance greased their days.

They say that fish is good for the brain,
but not while the soul still gasps in the shallows –
or is marshalled into the squabble of vivid air
and fatally caught by the simplest hook.

Their heads are made of dulling scales –
their eyes have sunk into the swallowing space.
It is the hollow revenge of dead-eyed fish –
haddock, cod or plaice.

Opening the Apocalypse Jar

Who says we should strive to live in peace –
we are all going to die at the curtained end.

We should start a war without delay
and contradict the hopes of millions of minds –

that flawless hope, found only in strategies
and in the futility that leads to an awkward place;

then hence, to something rare and special –
the honeyed fire of determined love.

A Nod's As Good As a Wink...
to a Blindfolded Poem

I have been paraphrasing Rod Stewart again, forgive me,
but an old wainscot will never let you down.
You just need to polish it with trust,
like everything you own. Especially if you wear it swell,
like the American dancer, Gene Kelly.
Everything was swell for him and Maggie Reynolds,
who gathered lilacs while Mae went west.
Gene, poor fool, was left swinging on the downtown crane,
like a chump, clinging in the rain.

It was good enough for Granddad though
(that old stuffed stoat who started to go brown)
following you, with unblinking eyes
as you went off to the dirty old town.
That same granddad, who sweat to death
in his guise of constant sorrow –
forever old, under the weight
of your brutal handbag ambitions.
He was as happy as a glad rag to stay home and worry.
He did not worry about rude epithets, though,
not that 'old fart of yours', who chose to die of work
because he did not die of war.
He never mentioned conflict much, saying:
'I don't want to talk about it,' while standing bravely
in his manicured garden and nailing his hand to a tree.

While you, being footloose and family free,
never led that blind horse past the toad of work –
not even for a Larkin.
'Have I told you lately,' he would say, 'that love hurts?'
Based on your oversight, or selfish attitude,

I have now prepared a dossier all about you,
in which every picture tells a Tory
how to be true blue – how to avoid becoming
as wet as the morning dew.
It is just not good enough, Iron Lady!
And I will be keeping an angel eye on you…
maybe more than one – maybe two shades of blue –
you're in my heart, you're in my jail –
it is the same thing.

They were wrong when they said 'Ain't love a snitch.'
It's a heartache – but can we still be friends?
In case not, I fooled around and fell in mud,
then made our rules perfect in your honour.
They clearly state that while you definitely may not,
Maggie may.

There is a rumour that Rod has Scot legs,
though he was born in London in 1945
(just in time to 'know no war',
as Pete Townshend told us, in his Who's Who).
As a granddad himself now,
Rod wades into the shallows of his later songs –
a welcome blond in a sea of grey.
He still has sex with tall girls he cannot reach,
and hardly cheek to cheek, he settles for Atlantic kissing.

'The first slut is the deepest,' said Granddad, always ready
to provide a dubious quip. 'And my bladder found a reason
to relieve that,' he continued, 'on getting an NSU at the
National Students Union in 1972.'

What were you thinking, Granddad?
The disease was apparently concealed in a song lyric
that was written above the stainless steel urinal.
'But cryptic, like...' he said, in a northern accent.
'I was pissing into what I thought was a steel guitar
with magical properties, supposed to make flatulence
sound like a mandolin wind,
but they couldn't change a thing... oh no... '

It was more a gale – and tonight's the kite the string broke,
falling back into a shower of stars
that lit our horoscopes with intimidating horrors.
Can someone please ask Maggie to make up?
We have to go failing in an hour.
In fact, I am failing now and it is painful.
I thought of suicide, but the best it could offer
was more death and that did not interest me.
I walked out, saying: 'Call that a life choice?
I'll stick with the rhythm of my heart. Bon voyage!'

Your Granddad committed suicide, you know,
indirectly though – more of a manslaughter
performed accidentally and against his better judgement –
no one thought to release him from the tree at sundown –
the one he had nailed himself to
as a brutal penance for surviving the war.
He had forgotten... for a very long time,
exactly where he was, and died –
some say, at the end of an extended fart,
Accompanied by a groan that meant pardon.
'He drowned in his own perspiration' said the report;
enough to fill three plastic handbags and a beer glass.

The funeral was footloose and fancy cakes
and there was never a dull dormant –

especially when Granddad, dressed in his gladdest rags,
rose from the dead via the rhythm of his heart –
'Yes, I was an old fart, but now I have a string section –
it's my way of giving,' he said, and began to sing:
'Tie a yellow Ribbentrop round an old oak tree'.
He sang it to be on the safe-side, the side of war,
and he embellished his words for future reference –
'Next time, use tape that glows in the dark,' he cautioned,
'no point having any more unnecessary fatalities
just because of a bit of twilight.'

No, an old raincoat will never let you forget.
As Gasoline Allison drives away, with the 'more fun'
of new blond days and experimental sex –
and with a baby crane to hoist her latest wig
out of the blues. Shouting and screaming, she was –
even her flag was cross, like Rod's is –
Yet her's, a background of very, very blue.
It still rippled proudly in the Saltire wind.
'Some guys have all the luck.' She screamed, in a broken
Dream, or was it dram? 'Where are you when I need you?
You are my reason to breathe, so stay with me!'
But instead, Rod went off for a night on the town.
Granddad had just been voted into Parliament, saying:
'That's what fiends are for, so let it be me!'
He bellowed out his policies, on moody Tuesday,
just like yon' Turks would have done.'

It had to be blue, didn't it? It had to be blue.
I wandered around and finally found,
someone else from The Who –
just to reconfirm a few more births and deaths.
'I was only joking,' said Rod 'when I cut across shorty.
By the way, do you think I'm sixty?'

Never Make an Exhibition of Yourself

The museum is dead now –
people always think museums are dead.
They are so sure of it they help them on their way,
using dark magic and the invocation of ignorance –
they willingly become the archenemy of display.
I suppose that makes my labours a success...
in an unsuccessful sort of way.
But the moment a museum is offered to the world
it has had its day.

It becomes nothing more
than periods of marketing and resurrection.
I called my museum Lazarus to save time
and added a teashop to save face.
People will always eat cakes and think about thinking.
Having explored the idea in a crumbling mind –
the small fee was a fearsome obstacle,
the stairs were unkind. Both were a challenge
they could neither surmount nor comprehend –
'the tea was nice though,' they said, 'dear friend,'
waving back into the blur of the street.

If you build a museum yourself, do not embrace
a modern approach – future implications merely confuse
and the future they want is not relevant here,
or remotely compatible with their wireless lives.
And do not attempt an historical setting,
people are well beyond the lessons of the past;
they trust nothing that is forced to endure – did not last.

No use either, are the printed balloons –

children will simply burst your name for fun.
You will seem nothing to them, but a conjuring trick –
drawn in the thin-air they imagined you were from.

You will suffer Mother Nightmare then –
the filmy horror of babies' lips, smearing panels
and teetering on their first liberation of slippery steps.
Welcome to the smudged blur of hell,
where the Dead sign in and the Devil paints their nails.
The café will become a nursery of prams
and the toilet facilities, used to give birth –
or just abused by the bowels of the passing street,
to whom a stolen piss is all you are worth.

Finally, resist the urge to become a theme park,
and certainly not during the panic of the very first day.
If you feel weakened and in need of redemption
go straight to the emergency helter-skelter and pray.

My museum was not killed by ignorant bliss,
it was wounded by its cohorts – apathy and fear.
And by the love it had for its cherished self –
refusing to allow history to disappear,
or worse, to slide into the timid muse
of modern embarrassments... that thinnest veneer.

> *If we said anything less we would be lying.*
> *A joke would help, and always does,*
> *if we are not too busy crying.*

A World of Farmed Exploitation

See the famous hosts of fallen angels –
each celebrity with a hand in our pocket.
Limited by guilt – some mentally unstable,
rocked by the weight of their hand-cuffed wealth.

Stop begging our forgiveness at charity's door,
with its implicit curse and simplistic response.
We are often pitifully wounded ourselves,
disarmed by the same constitutional stance.

Remember, it is we who know the price of everything –
a knowledge paid for by the trial of living.
Must our lives be condemned to the badgering stare
of your righteous ideas on the value of giving?

What is Current is Not

Life is merely light,
a glowing passage
through the night.
Shoring a past
that holds its faith,
and a pondered future,
never safe.
The flower is not
the moment gone,
or the minute
to look back upon.
We must illume with courage
and shield with hope –
this next precious second
of Avalon.

A Leap of Faith Left in the Dark

Church is consciously ignored these days.
Some who got married were heard to proclaim,
(while high on the enthusiasm of confetti and flowers)
that if it worked out they would visit again –
but were soon suspicious of their own married lives,
and also the lives of holy men.

Sex is a mortal sin, outside marriage,
and sometimes deemed that way within.
It is a marketing problem for the church to resolve –
a tattoo of snakes drawn under the skin.
It will never be welcome beneath the spire,
and never voiced by the rigid choir.

Religious men sometimes take missionary wives,
and sex is a leap of faith for them.
And in some religions a prohibited wife,
demands the celibate loins of priestly men.
It is judged to be wrong when sexual feeling
brushes the hair of spiritual healing.

Marriage is a hindrance to angelic prayer –
the conflict with chastity is plainly there.
So priests now stare at choirboys instead;
sometimes with a blatantly evil passion,
filling the whole parish with unholy contrition.

–'*The Beauty of Faith*': *Lourdes France 1990* –

Laughing at the Guru

The Guru sits beyond the world. And perfectly still –
a revised sportsman of another culture.
One that is not partial to physicality,
or demands brave heroes on their way to Mars.
They consider him a flame of enlightenment,
he who watches their tides and buoyant swell,
lifting the evergreen horizon like a revealing blind,
or bubbling up from a local well.

He watches our mountaineers, roped above him –
no higher than he, and climbing for nothing,
except perhaps a bitter pride they must long endure.
Yet nothing deeper than he himself had held plentiful –
a surplus, cupped and pure, in the palm of global hands;
washed away as worthless arrogance.

He sits higher than anyone,
having done all the things they think are existence –
those minimal things in vanity's chest –
a conceit that never accommodated a spiritual drawer.
The Guru is now a scrawny soul, fed on belief
and not much more –
yet plainly beloved beyond all reverence.

He passed into a new consciousness a while ago,
happy to be done with dreams and labours –
to have them gone, like an irritated guest,
who picks up their sack of contrition, and leaves –
seeking the burden of a widening vision.

The Guru sits still, elsewhere in the world –

preferably on the edge of things –
perhaps a silence on a mountain,
or a metaphysical, yet still dangerous ledge?

In western culture we have nowhere to climb
once we have ascended to the living edge.
Once we have turned that random page,
where social details do not take us seriously –
making us lords and ladies – figures of celebrity.

Our paragons are sportsmen now –
what could be worse?
Pushing their bodies with a secret dose –
gods and goddesses on their way to a nurse;
to the physical limit of pointless challenge,
all on behalf of a greedy, expanding universe.
(apostates will jog alongside the hearse)

Television is watched by bodies made of sweets,
that cannot resist the sins their new gods inspired.
They have dispensed with the metaphysical gods instead,
waving their religious teachings by.
(though I have seen their sportsmen gaze heavenward,
seeking favour from a conceit of empty sky)

Our gurus are progressively younger men,
with shaggy ideas and far less hair.
We grow tired of modelling a collusion with them –
it is a case of mistaken identity.

And when all our personal expeditions are over –
when the focus has found no five-leafed clover –

when we have explored every aspect of every detail,
to the point of becoming transfixed.
We will enter a time of transition and peace,
where nothing matters – and never will,
and the heart of all knowledge is poisoned and still.

We will watch the forgotten feature films then,
as we promised our youth, in the long winters gone.
They will absorb the truth of our Hollywood temple,
where pretence at knowing is stagnant applause –
a meek vibration to suit our fixity,
and the dreadful entrenching of bolted doors.

> *We are creatures of change,*
> *at home on the range.*
> *Riding with Roy Rogers.*
> *(who is acting strange)*

I prefer a true and earthly teacher, myself.
One who will understand that our laughter and scorn
is merely a display of the child, not yet overcome –
that we have not yet the means of transition from,
and are still waiting to be reborn.
And when we kneel in that giggling tide
we are only attempting the triumphs of our heroes –
the rewards they jumped higher and further for
without these blessed, broken knees;
without the gravity of life's piteous decay.
We take the world too seriously now,
but still find it all too shallow to breathe,
in those uneven depths of inquiry and play.

Steeped in Ashes

Everything changes in these subtle ways:
We enter the world and do the things we do
until we have done them far too much –
bending them from adventure into chore.
We feel the fun begin to flake –
not as focussed or free as it was before –
hardening in the lined palms of forecasting hands,
and in the still gaze of our purposed eyes.

Tomorrow's prophesy is a daunting hole.
The future is an awkward, deepening well.
The overkill of western society
has muffled us shut and made us ill.
I have no faith in augury now
and rely on the secrets of – who can tell?

Long before the end, our wheels will stop dead,
and even before then, they are thrown aside –
rusting companions in the garden shed.
We will shuffle then, still erudite, yet rude,
making a carer take our bitter arm
while smiling an awareness of our diminishing courtesy.
A random splash of profanity will do no harm.
(neither will their misdiagnosis wither our trust)

We can forget anything, in the sanctity of the town hall.
Or the library, where we nurtured a wordy lust.
Our necessary proposition has no other means
than to limp or crawl, or be purposely slow.
We will do anything to avoid the imminent arrival
of that proclaimed eternity – nowhere to go.

Hope in the Heart of Hatred

The world is cast in hatred – everywhere I look.
It grovels in the streets – in every twist and turn.
I think hope grows in heartache –
I think that's how it blooms.
I think that's how it seeds our trust
and how it saves the world.

Lady Stamford

Gone forever are the narrow lanes,
with comfortable cream cars
that drew the leaves with their breath.
Chasing echoes that will not fade,
until the next Spitfire
excites the safe old women
who guard England.

Gone are the shadows
'neath the wilting bough,
that spurned the raging summer
of swallow and swallowtail.
And gone is the comfort
of a window, ajar,
where the radio voice
trailed hours of secrets –
tuned well beyond emotion
or simple betrayal.

Gone forever is the brittle thatch,
where earwigs snoop and drop
to squirm in earth –
leaving the house alone.

And no more, will the stealthy sunlight
seat upon untainted soil,
to paint the cottage-garden scene
in colours of hollyhock, lavender
and simple green.

No longer will the kettle boil
in quite the same old way.

> *Now the past is sun-stripped paint,*
> *peeling the yellow gate from the honey days of youth.*
> *Now the past is re-enacted in the heavenly prayers*
> *of fifty-million thoughts of truth.*
> *Now the past is here today... then gone forever more...*
> *and never will it be that way,*
> *inside the edge of our English shore.*

Gone too, is the moisture
that could encourage these photographs to smile again.
A mantelpiece of human-beings,
caught in frames to warm the heart.
Viewed only when the fire is out.

Gone is the meadow where clouds sift the sky,
measuring dark and light, for both Kodak and men.
Travelling in pools, over fields and hills,
where grass blades cut the skin –
rewriting innocence with a virgin pen.

> *Now the past is sun-stripped paint,*
> *peeling the open gate from the heady days of play.*
> *Now the past is revisited in dreams,*
> *all holding the signatures of fifty-million names.*
> *Now the past is here today... then gone forever more...*
> *and never will it be that way,*
> *inside the edge of our English shore.*

But there is still the flower stall
on the High Street – now closed to traffic.
And people, happy with their feet...
and ferns for sale – and palms.
And sandwiches to match the price
of the proprietor's open arms.
And a wasp in the pastry window,
unsettled by the conundrum
of a sealed bell-jar.

But no longer will the kettle boil
in quite the same old way.

> *Now the past is sun-stripped paint,*
> *peeling the green gate from the rambling days of stiles.*
> *And a memory in the heavy hearts*
> *of fifty-million banished smiles.*
> *Now the past is here today... yet gone forever more...*
> *and never will it be that way,*
> *washing the edge of our English shore.*

Unless the sun shines on these perfect thoughts,
or startled by a compelling muse –
Lady Stamford, as she knows my soul,
has me thrown for a moment into an examining past...
never too far from our containing sea.
Where all the tides and memories that remain,
remain in me.

Her theatre is still the sunlit dust
that crumbles from a high, sandstone facade.

Her curtain is the cotton dress
that moves with her like a mouth and words.

You are the brown sugar of another age;
an actress on a well-worn stage.
A moving scene of elegant history,
now living in the better blood
of my other heart.

I lit a cigarette against the scorn of a modern stage
and blew the smoke across the footprints
of your trodden past.
The place where your heels had touched my earth
and it had shook the steps of eternity.
And dressed to kill, you killed the present
and filled the street with a bygone age.
An age of beauty – a nymph at war –
with a nineteen-forties stockings look
and the elegance of a full, dark seam.

You aimed to own a memory
of a world in turmoil – yet still in love.
A world kept secret by your lipstick mouth
and more peaceful than tomorrow's now.
An age where red would haunt out dreams,
yet leave us still at ease...

I could have crayoned that seam.
Let me draw the next one.
Please.

Index of Titles

Notes on the photographs

Before my 'rapture' by poetry in 1972 my artistic leanings had already been drawn towards creative photography – a way of seeing that has gripped my life ever since. Sometimes, taking a photograph seems a poetic act – almost a shorthand – in the same way that poetry can be the shorthand to life, or at least an unnecessarily verbose explanation of it. Equally the photographs accompanying these poems are not intended to be illustrations of them, they are merely images in their own existence that seem to have a symbiotic relationship – one that could be perceived as metaphysical at best – perhaps sharing a similar nature of being.

I take photography, and what it can achieve for demonstrating the various aspects of life, very seriously. I therefore feel the need to offer notes on some of these photographs, bearing in mind that they are presented here in a less than perfect reproduction setting – being no more than 'necessary ghosts'.

'Derelict House' and 'Closed' came from a period in the 1970s when I wandered in and out of old parts of my home town that were gradually being levelled.

'Bike on a Beach' was taken when I lived in a summer house belonging to my then girlfriend's family. They had bikes for the use of, and I rode up and down the beach in the winter of 1974.

The photograph taken inside the Palace of Versailles while I was on holiday in France in 1990, accompanies the poem: 'Where Does His Genius End?' The poem carries abstract references to previous occupants of the palace.

'Walking on Your Own Grave' is a poem about disregard for the environment, but there is nothing new in that. I was a lone environmental warrior fifty years ago, but nothing ever changes. Greed has the upper-hand and will burn everything. The two obsolete petrol pumps in the photograph were already well out of date in the 1970's and stood on that day as an emblem of decline, yet contradicted by the 'Opening soon!' sign in the window.

'Live Performance' – I called the hill with the silhouetted Horse Chestnut trees 'Wonder Land'. I could see it in the distance from where I lived, but I only ever visited once.

I passed the shuttered house bearing the name 'Maison De Petra' while hitch-hiking through France in 1972. I passed the 'Girl On A Wall' while driving through England in 1999. Hence my name seems lightly attached to both.

'The Apocalypse Jar' – more demolition from the 1970's. The poem relates to Pandora's box, which was originally described in the story as a jar.

The image of an old apple, left to rot on my windowsill in the 1970s. It is shared by two poems dealing with the subject of entropy. I call the wrinkled apple 'W. H. Auden'.

'The Beauty of Faith' – taken at Lourdes in 1990. I hope all the religious servants throughout the world believe in what they preach – and that God truly exists.

'It's a Wrap' was taken in Toulouse, southern France. I was lucky enough to arrive there in time to see a group of students wrapping a statue in pink and blue toilet paper. It accompanies the poem 'Laughing at the Guru'.

The array of bicycles share a page with a poem about youth, ageing, mobility, town-halls and libraries.

The picture of the old guy with the harmonica was taken in the shopping precinct of Lincoln in 1990. Looking back, it seems an act of hope, as much as anything I've ever seen.

In passing, I had noticed the old greenhouse for many years. One day, I decided to stop and take a photograph. There is something of the mood of 'Lady Stamford' about it – an embedded past.

A list of albums and song titles sung by
Rod Stewart
and paraphrased in the poem:
'A Nod's As Good As a Wink...
to a Blindfolded poem'

An Old Raincoat Won't Ever Let You Down
Everything I Own
You Wear It Well
Maggie May
Downtown Train
Dirty Old Town
A Man of Constant Sorrow
Forever Young
Handbags and Gladrags
This Old Heart of Mine
I Don't Want to Talk About It
Foot Loose and Fancy Free
A Nod's As Good As a Wink... to a Blind Horse
Have I Told You Lately
Love Hurts
Every Picture Tells a Story
True Blue
Morning Dew
Angel
Two Shades of Blue
You're in My Heart
Ain't Love a Bitch
It's a Heartache
Can We Still Be Friends
Fooled Around and Fell in Love
Hot Legs
Cheek to Cheek
Atlantic Crossing

The First Cut is the Deepest
Reason to Believe
Mandolin Wind
Tonight's the Night (Gonna Be Alright)
Sailing
Rhythm of My Heart
Never a Dull Moment
My Way of Giving
Gasoline Alley
Blondes Have More Fun
Baby Jane
The Blues
Some Guys Have All the Luck
When I Need You
Stay With Me
A night On the Town
That's What Friends Are For
Let it be Me
Ruby Tuesday
Young Turks
It Had to be You
Cut Across Shorty
Da Ya Think I'm Sexy

About the Author

Peter began writing poetry when he was studying graphic design and photography in Bristol during the early years of the nineteen-seventies, and although he showed a strong talent for art and creative photography, he decided in those formative days that he wanted to give his writing ability a fair chance. When the graphics course ended in 1973 he spent much of the rest of the decade doing just that, working on his first five writings, which included an epic poem of two-thousand lines. He says of that time: *"I was young, slightly adrift, but it was a wonderful period of personal development and creativity on many fronts."*

By the end of the seventies he decided to re-enter the world of commercial art, soon becoming highly successful and sustaining the position of creative director at a number of advertising and design agencies. By the late eighties though, he felt this full-on life was all-encompassing and he decided to become a freelance designer working for himself. This semi-controllable situation gave him time to pursue his natural commitment to writing, though to some extent he had maintained it throughout, as writing frequently reclaimed his attention. Many of his remarkable short stories and some other poems were written during this time, including a second epic poem, loosely set in the English seaside town of Scarborough.

Peter has continued to write ever since, but perhaps oddly for a writer, and someone so closely involved in the world of design and print, he never made much of an attempt to publish anything of his own, and says:

"I lingered on that road to nowhere only a short time, finding it a bleak and depressing experience. Back then, publishing was nothing like it is today; at best, I might have had an odd poem or two published in one of the small, infrequent magazines, and although these magazines were, and still are, brave undertakings and important to emerging poets and writers, I had no chance of seeing my work published as I intended it to be experienced. As a visual artist and designer, as well as a writer, it was very important to me to maintain creative control over my work – every aspect of my work is important in that sense. Making submissions was also very time consuming – I felt it actually disturbed my flow and I very quickly decided to keep my work to myself. Since then I have trodden this road again with greater perseverance and encouraging success."

Peter also had the everyday concerns of his clients to deal with, so as the millennium approached, and after ten years of service to freelance design, he moved to Derbyshire, where he created a small, private tourist venture that also had the support of a teashop. He was trying to find a stable income so he could continue to produce his creative work in the space around it – consequently, there was much more to come.

In 2007 he became involved in the world of digital art and 3D animation, a field in which he still occasionally works today using the art name 'e-brink'. He has also made short films, some of which are visual muses to readings of his favourite poetry by writers such as Emily Dickinson, T. S. Eliot, Philip Larkin and Byron. He says that reading other

78

poets work is a great lesson, and has helped him realise the same vocal possibilities for his own work. He has always had a great belief in the standard of his writing and has dedicated much of his life to it, hanging on to almost everything he has ever written. Now, not being as young and indifferent as he was, he feels more prepared to share his writing with the world. As a long-term partner I have seen almost all of it and it deserves to be out there. There will no doubt be further publications of his old and new work coming shortly.

Lara Newton 2021

Coming soon –

'GAIN OF FUNCTION'

One hundred and two poems

Printed by BoD™in Norderstedt, Germany